LIVING IN THE SOLUTION
NOT THE SITUATION

EVANGELIST
DOLORES M. JACKSON

Copyright © 2015 Delores Jackson

All rights reserved. No part of this book may be reproduced in any form or by any means, electronic or mechanical, including photocopying, recording, or by any information storage and retrieval system, without written permission from the author. This excludes a reviewer who may quote brief passages in a review. Unless otherwise noted, all Scripture quotations are from The Holy Bible, King James Version (KJV) and The New International Version (NIV)

Cover Design: Brittany Jackson

Published by G Publishing, LLC

Library of Congress Control Number:
    2014922879
ISBN: 978-0-9862379-2-8

Printed in the United States of America

Dedication

I dedicate this book to my Lord and Savior Jesus Christ for allowing and giving me the strength and courage to reach every child, boy or girl, lady or man that has been stricken with this terrible disease. We all can be soul survivors. I choose to live in the solution, not the situation. Just like any illness or disease it doesn't have to be a death sentence. It can be arrested with proper medication and education with the power of God.

Acknowledgments

I acknowledge my husband, for being very compassionate and understanding; for allowing God to use me in this way to give back to God and his people. I thank you for being my heavenly blessing.

Next I would like to acknowledge my four children: Gregory, Grant, Jeffery and Nicole. I thank the Lord, my God, that you all are my inspiration.

My parents, Johnny Matthews and Josephine W. Matthews, I thank you both for getting me ready for Sunday school and church every Sunday. I thank you for depositing love, respect and honesty in me at an early age in my life. Even though you have gone on with the Lord, I would like to say I love you both, and I still remember the many things you instilled in my life. I will see you again on the other side in that New Holy Jerusalem.

Table of Contents

Introduction 9

Chapter 1 11

The Journey 11

Chapter 2 22

Divine Opportunity 22

Chapter 3 36

Broken, Torn, but not destroyed 36

Chapter 4 55

Faith Under Fire 55

Daily Nuggets 74

There are seven stages to being a faith walker in God: 76

About the Author 79

Introduction

I know that this book will help young and old women and men across the globe in every walk of life. God gave me six words "you shall live and not die." From Psalm 118:7 I shall not die, but live and declare the works of the Lord.

Chapter 1

The Journey

My journey began in the summer of 2004. I had an appointment with my insurance agent to take an additional policy for security for my children. I got a statement in the mail that stated my insurance had been declined after eleven years with them. So when I got off the next day from work I went to talk to my agent and he instructed me to see a doctor right away to take a blood test. When I saw the details on the reading, I just knew that they were wrong.

So immediately I made a doctor's appointment the next day which was

Friday; my god-mother went with me. I didn't know what to do. She went with me to encourage and to support me. They called my name I started to run out the door, but I didn't. I went with the doctor into the examination room. The doctor came back with my results. She told me that my pap smear was normal but the blood was showing CB-4 count was coming up positive for HIV and viral load was high but not enough to start taking medicine at that time. I was so afraid I just kept saying to myself this cannot be true. My god-mother asked them could they do another test to be sure and behold it came back positive. I fell down to my knees with tears streaming down my face. I looked up at my god-mother saying this cannot be happening to me. I was torn up from the roof to the floor.

I asked the doctor what was the next step for me. She set an appointment for me with another doctor that specialized in that field to see the doctor every two months. I was still so frustrated and angry with myself,
I felt like I was at a point of no return. I felt like hurting myself.

The doctor wanted me to continue seeing him for a year. In the year of 2005 my CB-4 count and viral load hadn't change. The HIV virus at that point was still the same. I was so ashamed of myself. I couldn't make any sense of this because I was dating only one gentleman. I didn't even know how to tell him this had happened. I slipped twice with him and he had asked me to marry him. I just couldn't put it together. I eventually told him. He replied and said, "we will work through it." I thought that was my answer, but I was easily fooled.

I went to my spiritual leaders and told them what the doctor had said and they immediately prayed the prayer of faith over me. I remembered a bible verse that read, "Is there is any sick among you? Let him call for the elders of the church; and let them pray over him." (James 5:13)

I was really close to my spiritual leaders. For a long time I had this secret to myself. I rededicated my life back to God and I didn't slip anymore. I thought about the scripture Psalm 51:1-11. Have mercy upon me, O Lord, according to your loving kindness; according to the multitude of your tender mercies, blot out my transgressions. Wash me thoroughly from my iniquity, and cleanse me from my sin. For I acknowledge my transgressions: and my sin is ever before me. Purge me with hyssop, and I shall be clean. Wash me, and I shall be whiter than snow. Make me to hear joy and gladness; that the bones which you have broken may rejoice. Hide your face from my sins and blot out all my iniquities. Create in me a clean heart, O God; and renew a steadfast spirit within me. Do not cast me away from your presence and do not take your Holy Spirit from me.

At this time God spoke to me and said "you have found me to be a secret keeper." My spiritual leaders had told me it is by your faith in God that this disease will be destroyed. I remember what the scripture said in Hebrews 11:1. Now faith is the substance of things hoped for and the evidence of things not seen. So right then I had to have some now faith and I wanted it really bad.

I got busy studying God's word and applying his word in my life every second, minute, hour, and day until God calls me home. I did not know what to do with this, but I knew it was a unique thing and I wanted to please God. Whatever He said I was going to do it until one Sunday I went to church and the preacher was speaking about how God can love you in a bad situation. That sermon stuck with me for a long time. Then one night when I got ready to go to bed and finished my prayers I heard a small sweet voice speaking to me, "Trust me daughter; you shall live and not die." I thought about Proverbs 3:5-6. Trust in the Lord with all your heart and lean not to your own understanding; in all your ways acknowledge him and he shall direct your path.

I remember saying I will completely trust and depend on you Lord. After I said that it felt like something broke on the inside of me and tears began running down my cheeks. I tried to wipe them away but they were coming down like a stream running off the side of a river and they were warm like the rain coming out of a cloud on hot summer day. I had made a conscious decision in my life with the Lord. I was going all the way with my God and I knew without a shadow of doubt he had me. I had to step out into His word and believe it to the fullest. So In other words I had to step out into the deep water of faith where I had never gone, and I was not going to look back.

We easily say we believe in God, but when the tests come, they really show who you are and where you are in God. I thought about Revelation chapter 12:11 "And they overcame him by the blood of the Lamb and by the word of their testimony; and they loved not their lives unto death." God's word started coming up in me like flowing rivers that do not have an end. He spoke these words to me: "For God hath not given us a spirit of fear, but of power, and of love and of a sound mind. Be not thou therefore ashamed of the testimony of our Lord, nor of me his prisoner; but be thou partaker of the afflictions of the gospel according to power of God. Who hath saved us, and called us with an holy calling, not according to our works but according to His own purpose and grace, which was given us in Christ Jesus before the world began." II Timothy 1:7-9.

Everything we go through, God's word is there for us to bring us out of any situation. On the other hand, the word of God is our refuge and escape from a bottomless pit of no return. God showed me He was my secret keeper when I couldn't keep myself. I thank God for keeping my mind, heart, body, and spirit. To God be the glory. After God kept me and restored my body to full function, the man that I supposed to have married I discover was still married. God spoke to me, "Woman of God, go and sin no more and be free in me." I am free in God and all the ties of this world were broken off of me. God led me to the book of Isaiah 53:5. But he was wounded for our transgressions, he was bruised for our iniquities; the chastisement of our peace was upon him; and with his stripes we are healed. Right then, my mind and heart started coming together as one, then my spirit lined up with God's will, statutes, and his commandments in my life. I was just like a Mack truck (18 wheeler on the Interstate). I was on a mission and I wasn't going to let anyone or anything get in my way. I was non-stop in my mission to the broken hearted, wounded, despairing, woman or man, boy or girl. God had broken all chains and had set me free. I didn't understand all of it, I just went with the power of God; how he was directing and guiding my every footstep, and what a feeling with so much joy and excitement. Now I understand what Jeremiah was saying in chapter 20:8-9. "For since I spake, I cried out, I cried violence and spoil; because; the word of the Lord was made a reproach unto me, and a derision daily. Then I said, I will not mention of him nor speak anymore in his name. But his word was in my heart as a burning fire shut up in my bones; and I was weary with forbearing and I could not stay." When God has set you free and cleansed you from all filthiness and indecency, you just have to shout it out. I am free, I am free at last. I couldn't hold my peace.

Chapter 2

Broken, Torn, but not destroyed

God was showing and teaching me how to keep things about what I was going through. When you are being kept for the glory of God that is an awesome relationship you have with your heavenly father. I went to service one Sunday and heard the preacher that God can love you in a bad situation and love you just where

you are. I thought of Romans 5:8: "but God commanded his love towards us in that while we were yet sinners Christ died for us." Then I knew God was using this situation to be a divine opportunity for is glory. I read Mark 5:25, "and a certain woman which had an issue of blood twelve years. And had suffered many things of many physicians and had spent all that she had; and was nothing bettered, but rather grew worse." Then it says in verse 27, "when she had heard of Jesus' coming, she pressed behind him and touched his garment. Verse 28, "for she said, if I may touch but his clothes, I shall be whole. Verse 34 and he said unto her;" Daughter thy faith has made thee whole; go in peace and be whole of thy plague.

God demonstrates his own love toward me while I continue trying to do it on my own. God said, "Daughter here is my hand. I will never let you go. I love you just the way you are and I am going to take this bad situation and turn it into something beautiful. When people pick up this book and begin reading, they will not see you, but see me. Just like the woman with issue of blood it was just a temporary situation until I tapped into the real source of power which is the Lord Jesus Christ. Remembering what John 15:13says, "Greater love has no one than this, that a man lay down his life for friends.

God knows that we cannot change our situation or course of life without him. That's why God gave me the title for this book, (Living in the solution and not the situation), and the solution is in the Almighty Lord Jesus Christ. Philippians 4:13 says, "I can do all things through Christ which strengtheneth me," With his word and his precious Holy Spirit, I am victorious and not a victim through Him.

Watch what you say: We need to watch what we say and how we say it, especially when we are saying it to the Lord. I remember I made a vow unto God when I was living in sin. I asked the Lord to take the desire for drinking from my lips and I would do the right thing. God delivered me and saved my mind and body from drinking. It has been over 23 years clean and sober from any kind of alcoholic beverage or any kind of drugs. I know without a doubt that God did this for me at this point in my life. I was so tired of being sick and disgusted with myself. I just wanted out. I was so sincere with myself and God. I remembered reading Deuteronomy 23:21, "when you make a vow to the Lord your God, you shall not delay to pay it; for the Lord your God will surely require it of you and it would be sin to you." Verse 22 reads, "But if you abstain from vowing, it shall not be sin to you." Verse 23 states, "That which has gone from your lips you shall keep and perform for you voluntarily vowed to the Lord your God, what you have promised with your mouth." I told God I was not going to get in any more trouble, and I kept my promise. But what little I knew, God was looking at a bigger picture, my soul, not just my body.

Many times God has spoken things unto me to say or to go somewhere. I would hold back on God because even though I was grown in body, my mind was not to the level of maturity that I could comprehend what God was telling or asking me to do. We serve a mighty big God who sits high and records everything you say and do. I was so ashamed. I kept this secret for a long time. See the enemy has traps already set up for us, but we have to be smarter than him. I tried to get out of doing what God had asked of me. See when you try to run from God he always has another avenue for you to run to, and it was straight to Him. I have always thought I wasn't good enough for anyone until I met my real Secret Keeper (Jesus).

I had to come to a mountain of decisions because what I was experiencing, no one taught me about life. Life experience taught with the protection of a powerful God watching over me. I thought about the prophet Jonah. How God instructed him and assigned him a task to go down to Nineveh. I really didn't understand the whole concept of what God was getting me prepared to do. I was scared. I didn't trust anybody in the setting of church. Everybody was talking the word, but their lives did not add up to the Word. At that point in my life, I was very confused. Then God started speaking with me in dreams. He was letting me know he was still here, and told me to look to Him. I remembered Psalms 37:1: "Do not fret because of evil doers nor be envious of the workers of iniquity, for they shall soon be cut down like the grass, and wither as the green herb."

I ran from God a long time. I did not want to preach God's word. The more I ran, I always ended up in church in the presence of pastors, apostles, overseers, prophetesses, teachers and evangelists. The weird thing was they liked me and wanted me around them.

I didn't have to do anything extra to be accepted; they took me as I was. I asked myself what was going on. I told God I can't win in what I am doing so I will join forces with your true believers of the faith. I found out quickly when God called and chose me for this assignment. You may run for a while, but you cannot hide. Jonah 1:2 "Arise go to Nineveh , that great city and cry against it for their wickedness is come before me." Verse 3, "Jonah arose to flee to Tarshish from the presence of the Lord. He went down to Joppa and found a ship going to Tarshish: so he paid the fare thereof and went down into it to go with them unto Tarshish from the presence of the Lord." Verse 4, "But the Lord sent out a great wind on the sea, and there was a mighty tempest on the sea, so that the ship was about to be broken up."

See, disobedience will cause you to suffer more than you should. I did not want to accept the calling of evangelizing. I thank my Lord and Savior even though I disobeyed him, he chastened me with his love and he taught me why I had to accept this assignment. Nobody can do it the way God does. He love me so much, he gave me another chance. Then I started to understand his instructions and plans for my life. When you are disobedient to God your disobedience can endanger the lives of innocent people. I was walking in disobedience as Jonah. God knew that the enemy has traps set up for us. Instead of running away from God I should have been more focused on running to God, and running from the enemy. Believe me when I say I ran so hard I fell right in the enemy's trap and camp. God allowed me to fall into the enemy's hand because he knew that I needed him more than he needed me. When you are flat on your back everything and everybody is against you. There is only one power, one source, and one solution that can bring you out calling on the name of Jesus. God will allow you to be just where you want to be until you get so sick and tired of it that you are no longer in control of it. I remember I was so drained and exhausted, I needed God to rescue me. I found out that after all the running I did, He was right there all the time. I thank God for all he taught me during my period of disobedience. If the enemy had never tormented me I would never have received the understanding of God's power and the great love he has for me. I totally accepted God's call on my life in the year 2005. I have been running the race for the Lord ever since. I had to find out just like Jonah. God prepared a great fish to preserve Jonah and deliver him on dry land. He used the fish to preserve Jonah and he used HIV to preserve me and keep me so I wouldn't look back. The fish and its divinely appointed rendezvous with the sinking prophet became a powerful reminder to Jonah of the sovereignty of God in every circumstance.

I got sick with HIV, but in the process God preserved my body and mind for the Lord. What the enemy meant for my bad, God turned around for my good. Believe me, there is always something out there bigger and stronger than you and the only one that can help us is our Lord and Savior Jesus Christ. When God calls you to do an assignment, just do it and do not try to make deals; or say I hear you God, but later. That is not how He works. I didn't want to write this book, but this is an assignment from the Lord. He has instructed me what to write. I AM HIV FREE today. I know that this book will help someone come out of their dungeon or chains that are holding them down. Whatever the case may be, God is the only one that can loose all shackles and chains from your life. I had to tell the truth so this will help someone be free today. Maybe your case or status is different from mine, but God is the answer. Just remember that anything that holds you back and keeps you from serving totally is a stronghold of sin. Isaiah 10:27 states "and it shall come to pass in that day that his burden shall be taken away from off thy shoulder, and his yoke from off thy neck, and the yoke shall be DESTROYED because of the ANOINTING."

I remember John 9:31 Now we know that God heareth not sinners: but if any man be a worshipper of God and does His will, him he heareth." I thank God every for his unfailing love and grace that when I wanted to give up on my life He stepped in and told me that's why I went to the cross and laid down my life for you; that you may have a chance to live life to fulfillment. That is so awesome to me. Everything that we struggle with or experience, God has already paid in full by the shedding of Jesus' blood. The scripture says in 1 John 4:4, "Ye are of God, little children, and have overcome them: because greater is he that is in you than he who is in the world." That lets me know as long as we have him in our equation (life) we can overcome any obstacle in our lives. Romans 8:37 Yet in all these things we are more than conquerors through him who loves us. I look like the word of God rose up in me. Scriptures started coming from every part of the bible. During that time He wanted me to know without a doubt He still had me and loved me and wasn't going to let me go. To God be the glory.

Chapter 3

Divine Opportunity

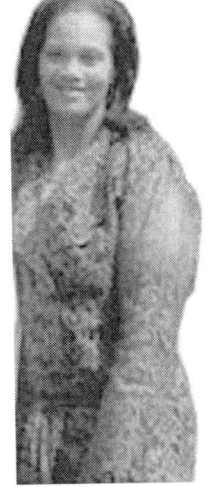

–"I shall not die but live and declare the works of the Lord." Psalm 118:17 Even though the enemy thought he had me, yes for a little while, God prevailed at the end. I started running hard for the Lord, doing everything I thought I could do. I got involved in nursing home ministry, teaching Sunday school to the children's class, and adult class also. I knew the only way for me to come out on top was to fight back and take back what was mine in the first place.

We, as a generation, give too much over into the hands of the enemy. That's why he plays with us. God birthed us with us with talents and gifts and when things do not pop up right away for us, we get impatient with the matter and try to fix it. Then we get upset or discouraged with ourselves. It is okay to be in a spot of dryness (still) it's not that God does not hear us; it's just not our season to receive that harvest at that particular time. Yes I was broken and torn, but I helped initiate the problem and the Lord knew I was playing with fire. No one could tell me in a million years I would end up in this situation. There was still a chance for me. I cried out to the Lord so many times like the little boy crying wolf.

I really believe the reason that I didn't get destroyed was because my repentance was sincere. I kept believing in God's word and working doing the things of God such as bible study, Sunday school, and whatever needed to be done, I stepped up and did it. In case God came at that particular time in my life I was living like it was my last day.

I wasn't asking much from God at this time in my life. I thought of James 4:17, "Therefore to him who knows to do good and does not do it, to him it is sin." I knew God would heal me, not in my time, but in His time. I had accepted if he didn't heal my body from HIV, I was ok with it. I would rather go to heaven with a thorn in my side than to lift my eyes in hell. I had accepted many decisions in my life about my health. God still wanted to use me for his glory. In other peoples' eyes I was a nobody, but one day God took this nobody and turned me into a diamond for his kingdom. Because of my honesty and the love I have for God and God's people, working through my situation kept me humble and submissive to God. I found peace through a bad and deadly situation but through it all God had my back.

Whatever you are going through in life, you can still hear God's still quiet, soft voice speaking to you in your situation. My natural body was torn up from the bottom to top. It was so extraordinarily awesome that God did not allow anyone to see the breakouts on me. God protected and shielded me that not could see the ulcers and legions that this disease can cause. They were there but no one could see them. What a mighty God we serve.

I can't change what happen back then, but I can surely move forward with God. That is why God had me to write this book so He can reach so many people because He is the ultimate healer. HIV is shocking. It carries a stigma. It is shameful in the eyes of man. I know that this book is a way for me to reach out to someone to let them know that they are not alone. Having a network or a circle of supporters you can trust or even a person, helps to ease a lot of pain and frustration. I was time to get my life together, HIV or AIDS was not something that was going to break me or take me out. I started going out speaking on this disease to anyone that has an ear to listen. I wanted to give back that which was so rightly given to me, another chance at living a clean life. I choose to live beyond HIV with the help of the almighty God.

The word of God says in Philippians 4:13, "I can do all things through Christ which strengthens me." II Peter 1:3-4 says, "his divine power has given to us all things that pertain to life and godliness through the knowledge of him who called us by glory and virtue, by which have been given to us exceedingly great and precious promises, that through these you may be partakers of the divine nature."

These scriptures that God laid on my heart will comfort us in times of trouble. II Corinthians 1:4 "Who comforteth us in all out tribulation, that we may be able to comfort them which are in any trouble, by the comfort wherewith we ourselves are comforted of God." Verse 5 continues, "For as the sufferings of Christ abound in us, so our consolation also aboundeth by Christ." As the God of comfort, he ministers to his people in every situation. Large or small instances of trouble in the lives of God's people are met with encouragement. He proves himself faithful to his people by acting in this way. God gave his son in death for us. Surely he won't abandon his people. Romans 8:32-34 reads, He that spared not his own Son, but delivered him up for us all, how shall he not with him also freely give us all things? Who shall lay anything to the charge of God's elect? It is God who justifieth? Who is he who condemneth? It is Christ, who died, yea rather, that is risen again, who is even at the right hand of God; who also maketh intercession for us." We who have received God's comfort become the agents of his comfort to others. If comfort comes from the God of comfort, then it surely comes through Christ.

When we connect with someone who is experiencing in the present what we have experienced in the past, we sense an immediate closeness with that person. God's love and comfort are made real and tangible as his people become vessels that carry to others what God has already given to them. However; we will find ourselves prepared to help others see how God's grace works even in the midst of difficult times or circumstances as we experience God's love through others in the midst of our own suffering. Experiencing what Christ experienced as well as receiving all that Christ gives. God is faithful to those who suffer for being united with him. God's comfort and encouragement are greater than suffering we have experienced. II Corinthians 4:8 reads, "We are trouble on every side, yet not distressed, we are perplexed but not in despair; Verse 9 continues, Persecuted, but not forsaken; cast down, but not destroyed;" The NIV finishes the chapter with, ¹⁰ We always carry around in our body the death of Jesus, so that the life of Jesus may also be revealed in our body. ¹¹ For we who are alive are always being given over to death for Jesus' sake, so that his life may also be revealed in our mortal body. ¹² So then, death is at work in us, but life is at work in you.

¹³ It is written: "I believed; therefore I have spoken."[b] Since we have that same spirit of[c] faith, we also believe and therefore speak, ¹⁴ because we know that the one who raised the Lord Jesus from the dead will also raise us with Jesus and present us with you to himself. ¹⁵ All this is for your benefit, so that the grace that is reaching more and more people may cause

thanksgiving to overflow to the glory of God.

We must stand with Christ. The cross teaches us about our suffering and God's comfort. Christ suffered on behalf of us. He took on himself the punishment that we deserve. He suffered so that we can have God's blessing. The things we experience in suffering for God, he allows so that the lowest place in our lives, with the hard times, are to merely toughen us up. These things we experience and go through are not to break us, but to build us up in Christ Jesus.

When we go through the molding and breaking period, we can minister to the broken hearted and the ones who are down in the valley of despair. In II Corinthians, the fourth chapter I looked at Paul's life and all the persecution that he went through where he experienced ups and downs working with new believers at the church of Corinth. He experienced a lot of things and became all the more able to minister the gospel to hurting people to be a vessel for God. God has disciplined and developed me to endure as a prayer warrior for others. God enabled me to overcome hardships or obstacles in my life to provide a seasoned example to others who are hurting and suffering. He is building and shaping us to be living vessels of his mercy and comfort to people from all walks of life. God is using our scars, tribulations and sufferings as examples of Christ's body in the world that others may see the work of the shedding of the blood on the cross was real.

My suffering is a sign of being in relationship united with Christ. God will provide everything that I need to endure and grow and become the person whom God called me to be in him God's power can shine brightly in dark situations when there is no way out in human terms. The almighty sovereign God made an escape for me. Think of Jesus; how no one's situation looked more helpless than his. He was abandoned by his followers, arrested, condemned, publicly tortured and killed by the imperial Roman authorities. Among Jesus' own words was a cry of anguish that God had abandoned him. Matthew 27:46, "and about the ninth hour Jesus cried with a loud voice saying E'-li, E'-li, la'-ma – sa-bach'-tha-ni? That is to say My God, My God, why hast thou forsaken me?

Yet God raised Jesus from the dead, victorious over death and all his enemies. In the death and resurrection of Christ, God shows his people that he is faithful to them not by preventing every instance of suffering, but by giving them his resurrection life in the very midst of suffering. Our weakness is the setting in which God demonstrates his supreme power. God is the foundation of every believer's confidence in every situation. When you are going through or in trouble, always look up. Psalms 121:1-2 says, "I will lift up my eyes unto the hills, from whence cometh my help. My help cometh from the Lord, which made heaven and earth."

Lord, I want to be able to say I have fought a good fight. I have finished the race. I have kept the faith and there is laid up for me a crown of righteousness that you will give to me and all who love you on that final day when we go to be with you. (II Timothy 4:7-8) Because of you, I can "glory in tribulations knowing that tribulation produces perseverance; and perseverance, character, and character, hope," Romans 5:3. I know I will never be disappointed by putting my hope in you because your love has been poured out in my heart by the Holy Spirit which is in me, who is the guarantee of my great future with you. Yes I know the enemy comes to kill, steal and destroy, but God comes to give me life more abundantly. "The Lord is good, a stronghold in the day of trouble; and he knows those whose trust is in him," Nahum 1:7. I know God does not want a part-time partnership. He wants a full-time relationship with me. God is tired of us wanting to get our thrills from him without putting on the ring of commitment. Some are more excited with feelings than the glory of God. Godly relationships are not based on feelings, but facts. As we made the choice to turn away from God's face at the mountain, every other commitment in our lives begins to deteriorate and fall apart. God is calling me to higher level of commitment in him. Spiritual leaders have always taught us that God doesn't just want a visitation, he wants a habitation. God wants us to have a consuming desire for him. God is calling me to a new level of intimacy with him because that is the only way I can get my divine healing. I have to grow closer to him in his presence and become stronger than I could ever imagine.

I started falling in love with God, the Son, and the Holy Spirit. David wrote in Psalm 1:3 that he should "be like a tree planted by rivers of water that brings forth its fruit in its season, his leaf also shall not wither and whatever he does shall prosper." If I was going to prosper and be in good health I had to do it the way God instructed me to do it. At that time in my life I became a disciple for the Lord and not a member for man. God instructed and directed me how to be a disciple.

Discipleship means to learn and to follow him. "Come to me, all you who labor and are heavy laden and I will give you rest," Matthew 11:28-29 "take my yoke upon you and learn from me. I am gentle and lowly in heart. You will find rest for your soul." Verse 30 continues, "for my yoke is easy, and burdens is light." Being a disciple is to first hear, listen, learn and follow, and be a doer of God's instructions. I got to a point in my life where I didn't care about what someone thought about me; it didn't matter anymore because I knew God loved me. He loved me and forgave me if no one else did. I thought about Matthew 5:6, "Blessed are they which do hunger and thirst after righteousness: for they shall be filled." For the first time in my life I knew what real love was. Real love does not judge you or condemn you; instead it picks you up and embraces you; it encourages and supports you. See my friend, if I lose you along the way, I have just lost a friend, but if I lose my God, or Jesus, his word, my savior and my greatest friend, I will lose my life eternal and everlasting. God is my everything. Shout it out for Jesus. I can't allow any temporary situation to mess me up eternally. Mark 8:34-37 says: "Whosoever will come after me, let him deny himself, and take up his cross, and follow me.³⁵ For whosoever will save his life shall lose it; but whosoever shall lose his life for my sake and the gospel's, the same shall save it.³⁶ For what shall it profit a man, if he shall gain the whole world, and lose his own soul?³⁷ Or what shall a man give in exchange for his soul?"

See my friends, I was torn up and my heart seemed like it was broken into tiny pieces. I had come to a hard decision in my life. If I was going to be free and have peace, I had to start denying myself the carnal things of this world and pick up my cross and follow God and do as he instructed me.

Yes I was torn, broken but, not destroyed and I know all that I have been through will help some man, boy, girl or woman one day because I have been chosen and called by God to tell this life event that happened to me. God brought me out of the horrible pit where I once was. Just don't stop at believing only.

I thank my almighty God for what I went through because I wouldn't be who I am today. I am a strong, beautiful and blessed woman.

Chapter 4

Faith Under Fire

From the year of 2005 to the year of 2008 I had to let God be the only man in my life if I was going to be a true conqueror in Christ Jesus. I wasn't going to let anyone, or any situation, hinder my growth with my God. I remembered talking with my oldest son; he was so concerned about me. I had to reassure him, "Baby, mommy is not going anywhere yet. I have too much to do for the Lord." God started ministering to me in dreams in the midnight hour. He was building me as my body was sleeping, but my spirit was quite the opposite. God would instruct guidelines to me while my body was getting the proper rest. Mark 14:38 reminds us to "watch ye and pray lest you enter into temptation." The spirit truly is ready, but the flesh is weak."

See I had an extremely hard job. I worked up to 16 hours a day, then I had to come home and do my other job; the unique job of being a mother to my four wonderful, amazing children. So many people (co-workers) wondered how I could work all those hours and still keep it together and not have a man in my life. But I did have a man in my life. His name is Jesus Christ, the son of the living God.

I knew what I was feeling and going through was a divine wilderness experience in my life at that time. I just wanted God and my children because they were my inspiration and my stepping stones to go higher in Christ. See, being a mother to my children had been an extraordinary accomplishment in my life, and to have worked over 23 years at the same job has been an extraordinary experience for me. But, being a servant for Christ Jesus is a phenomenon in my life to be all above and get the assignment completed. Jesus was teaching me, and showing me that all I ever needed was him. He started giving me more dreams, speaking to me in them, and visions to encourage protect and warn me about different people that I was working with; who were surrounding me inside the work place and in the house of prayer.

Not everyone around you is there for your good. I didn't quite understand exactly what was going on or what was taking place. But I do know I wasn't going to turn around or look back to ask the questions. I just allowed God to take me through the process. God had all of my attention. The question he asked me was "How bad do you want me?" And I answered and said,

"I do not know how to balance my life without you in every area, but you do. So here I am, take me and do your will, sir."

God was building me and making me all over again. He told me "You are a building under construction". My foundation was solid, but the siding wasn't firm enough. What I am saying is what my parents had deposited into me wasn't enough for me to stand against the traps of the enemy.

I lost my parents at the age of twelve. Some of my siblings had to pick up and finish the assignment that was once started. I asked God how I was going to be a complete building with no earthly parents to teach me? At that time God said to me, "I made the heaven and earth, man and woman and breathed life into them." That was enough for me.

His voice began to be so strong until I could hear from God so clearly that it was like seeing through a crystal glass. It was clear to me. I was taking God at his word, seeking him, fasting, and following down on my knees and even threshing in his presence; waiting patiently for him to speak to me. I didn't have anything on my mind but God and my children. God came first, then my children, then my job. I had completely stepped out of equation and totally surrendered unto God, and I was glad I had given myself over to him entirely.

See people, God was restoring me back to the first, which is his love. Restoration is not easy. It may not come all at once. It may not come quickly. The disciples of Jesus required every day with Jesus for years to prepare them for their journey. Let us not be unduly discouraged if the transformation we long for does not take place immediately; let us feel the need and lay it to heart. Let us continue to be instant in prayer. Let us stand fast in faith. See, cleaving to Jesus with persistence and purpose of heart can never be put to shame. The hour will surely come when, if we behave perseveringly in him, out of our hearts will flow rivers of living water.

In 2007, a young man came into my life. He wasn't just an ordinary man; he was a worshipper of Jesus Christ. We had known and worked together for 10 years. He saw something different in me. I didn't give him a second thought or look because I was not sure if he was real or not. I thought it was too good to be true and I knew the devil had traps set for me. II Corinthians 11:13-14 reads, 13 For such are false apostles, deceitful workers, transforming themselves into the apostles of Christ. 14 And no marvel; for Satan himself is transformed into an angel of light. I was afraid. He was speaking the right words and speaking the right language, but I thank God for the Holy Spirit living inside of me. (My light bulb switch came on which was the Holy Spirit of God). Don't move too quickly, but be still. God was allowing me to know what I was feeling was okay. Daughter, I have rebuilt and restored you. Now what are you going to do with this matter at hand. I said nothing because you haven't told me anything about this. God you haven't spoken to me about this young man so why should I dwell on this matter.

(Smile; thanking God in advance) See God was letting me know I have the equipment to pass this test or fail it. (God gives us choices.) Remember, I belong to God. So see, I wasn't even thinking on my own, the very thoughts and deeds belong to him.

Luke 12:7 says, But even the very hairs of your head are all numbered. Fear not therefore: ye are of more value than many sparrows. All I ever wanted in life was to be great and rich in God. I want my life to speak for me. I had asked something of God in secret about something. No one knew but God.

Matthew 6:6 says, But thou, when thou prayest, enter into thy closet, and when thou hast shut thy door, pray to thy Father which is in secret; and thy Father which seeth in secret shall reward thee openly. And the request came just like I asked from God. In the year 2008, this young man asked to go to church with me on Sunday. I met him at the church that Sunday. I introduced him to my spiritual leaders and some of my brothers and sisters in the body of Christ. We started having bible study with each other visiting each other's church. The young man was always a friend to me. Then one day he asked me about marriage. I turned and looked at him and said, "What about it and smiled". Then I told him I was already married to God and He was enough and plentiful.

He had the nerve to quote a scripture from the bible that says God didn't want man to be alone. I was like, what? That is not what it says. In Genesis 2:18 it says "and the Lord God said, it is not good that man should be alone. I will make a help meet for him." (Helper comparable to him) Then verse 22 says, "And the rib, which the Lord God had taken from man, made he a woman, and brought her unto the man."

When I finished saying that to him, he realized I was nothing to play with and that I was serious about my relationship and habitation with God. That brother just smiled and didn't know what to say, but to agree with the truth. So to make a long story short, that same young man went and asked my spiritual leaders for my hand in marriage. And guess what, that is what I asked in secret of God that if any man wanted to marry me, he would have to go to my spiritual leaders and ask their permission first. I told him what the doctor had said about my health status. I was totally honest with him and he replied and said, I know you are a woman of prayer, supplications, and faith.

I shouted and praised God all day long. My children thought I had lost my mind. I believe the marriage took place because of my obedience, submission, and total surrender to God. July 12, 2010 I went back to the doctor and he told me they couldn't find any trace of Immunodeficiency Virus in my blood. I asked him to do another test and he did. In the next three months, the test results stated untraceable. I was in good health and God dropped all charges against me and set me free in Him. Believing his words in Isaiah 53:5 says, But he was wounded for our transgressions, he was bruised for our iniquities: the chastisement of our peace was upon him; and with his stripes we are healed. I am just like the man in John 9 who God totally healed from blindness. People were astonished and didn't believe him. Some of you will believe and some won't, but nevertheless, I know that God did this for me because he loved me so much that He was bruised and beaten for my iniquities. I am HIV free and my husband never had the virus.

I give God the glory. I am still in love with God, happily married and content with my loving husband, and we are both serving God and God's people. Shout it out for divine healing that I am HIV free and not destroyed. Isaiah 40:31 reads, "But they that wait upon the Lord shall renew their strength; they shall mount up with wings as eagles; they shall run, and not be weary; and they shall walk, and not faint." God showed me how to mount up and have wings as an eagle. He showed me how to fly over my situation and not beneath it. If you don't, you will not be able to conqueror your issues in life. God showed me how to mount up, climb and how to get up and stay up and not look back Like Psalm 121:1-2; "I will lift up mine eyes unto the hills, from whence cometh my help. My help cometh from the LORD, which made heaven and earth." In order to stay mounted up over your situation, your mind has to be heavenly conscious of the master himself, which is Christ Jesus. It is time mount up and rise above your issues with God's help.

God showed me how dissect each word in Isaiah 40:31:

Run: moving faster than walking, but easily and freely to complete a race.

Weary: tired or worn out.

Walk: to go on foot at a moderate pace as God directs.

Faint: feeling weak and dizzy. Do not be in a hurry but take your time.

Put it all together and make it work to your advantage. He shall charge and renew your strength and power. Soar on wings of God like an eagle. See, eagles represented leadership and power. The eagle is used figuratively to describe God's protection and care. After God brings you out of the horrible pit, into the marvelous light, he girds you up and teaches you how to fly in him. God is pictured as a loving parent who redeems and protects his people even as the parent eagle cares for her young. Ephesians 6:10 says, "Finally, my brethren, be strong in the Lord; and in the power of his might." God want us to triumph over all of our obstacles through him. My wing of strength is knowing who I am in God, and receiving the wisdom and knowledge of God. In I Peter 2:9 reminds you, "But you are a chosen generation, a royal priesthood and an holy nation, a peculiar people; that you should shew forth the praise of him who hath called you out of darkness into his marvelous light." I thank God that He didn't give up on me and gave a chance to make it right. "The Lord is my light and my salvation; whom shall I fear? The Lord is the strength of my life, of whom shall I be afraid," (Psalm 27:1)

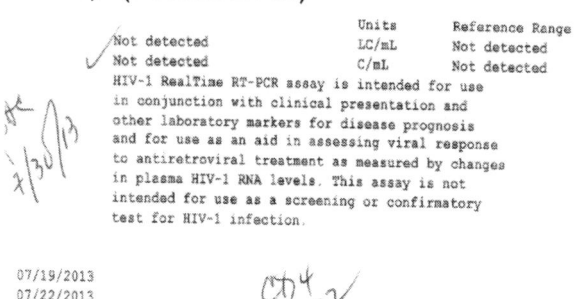

This is the result of faith under fire. I am a strong woman of beauty, highly favored, and blessed. I am a woman of strength who kneels in prayer to keep myself in strength. I am a bold woman today and not afraid of anything or anybody. I am woman of strength who shows courage in the midst of suffering. Because I give my best to anyone, I refuse to let anyone or anything get the best of me. I am a woman who has made many mistakes, but I refuse to let my mistakes make me. I have learned to capitalize on my mistakes knowing that God can use them to bless me. I am a woman of integrity and confidence.

Today I am not walking in my situation; I am living in my solution, which is the Lord Jesus Christ. This is why I am living in my solution and not walking in my situation any longer. Because Romans 8:37-39 says: Nay, in all these things we are more than conquerors through him that loved us. 38 For I am persuaded, that neither death, nor life, nor angels, nor principalities, nor powers, nor things present, nor things to come,

[39] Nor height, nor depth, nor any other creature, shall be able to separate us from the love of God, which is in Christ Jesus our Lord.
PRAISE GOD.

Daily Nuggets

A. Examine yourself, in your mind, body, and soul.
B. The more you surrender yourself to God, the more his love will flow through you and out to others.
C. You will realize that God is walking you through your storm.
D. By learning how to renew your mind on a daily basis, your life will be forever changed.
E. You will be able to sense the difference between good and evil thoughts.
F. God will give you a path of direction for supernatural discernment in things you never would have experienced on you own.

G. You will experience a newness of praise and worship in your life.
H. No matter where you have been or what you have done, you know that God loves you and will never leave you or forsake you.

There are seven stages to being a faith walker in God:

1. Survival refers to your ability to function as a new Christian, growing spiritually and living victoriously.

2. Honeymoon stage: you are happy and preoccupied with your new relationship with Christ.

3. Fight stage, the old habits and feelings may begin to creep back into your life.

4. Doubting stage. You may begin to wonder what salvation is all about. You will feel a need for more information.

5. Panic-search-for-truth-stage. You may begin to ask yourself how do I decide what truth is and feel confused.

6. Silent Christian: It may become easier and easier to remain silent and not tell others about Christ.

7. Quiet time: Each day you must find a time to be alone with Christ and you will be pleased with the results of doing so. You will be a healthy faith walker in God.

Books I like to read:

Holy Bible NKJV

Experiencing God through Prayer by Jeanne Guyon

Prayer and Spiritual Warfare by Charles Spurgeon

Humility by Andrew Murray

Walking in Your Destiny by Juanita Bynum

My study material: Comparative Study Bible by Zondervan

Amplified Study Bible by Zondervan

Zondervan NIV Matthew Henry Commentary.

Strong's Dictionary by Strong

About the Author

Evangelist Delores Jackson is an intercessor, highly gifted discerning and compassionate about things of God and for the people of God.

She is a very humble and uplifting prayer warrior, and a teacher: She has conquered many obstacles in her life by faith in God. In the face of trials and tribulations you will always hear the words "I'm good." In times of sickness, you will not hear her complain but you will hear her say "I'm good."

She is a woman who totally believes in God's word. She is committed and consistent to the ministry for God, known by her favorite confession "I am good."

She is a loving and devoted wife, mother of five beautiful children and grand-mother of seven bundles of joy.
Where others have given up, she

encourages others by her confession of faith "I'm good."

Her undoubting faith in God her praise and worship in spite of is a testimony of real faith in God.

She is a motivational speaker in parts of central Georgia. She has conducted and taught classes and workshops on substance abuse, AIDS awareness, health fair explosion, and hosted a local women's conference "Women with a Purpose."

She has served as an adult and youth Sunday school teacher and a choir evangelist.

The revelations presented in her first book are a road map to a faith walk with Christ. It will encourage you and help you in building your faith in God.

She is a woman who hears, listens, and walks with God hand in hand - a woman who walks with purpose.

Special Thanks To:

My spiritual leaders. Apostle William Basby and First Lady Michelle Basby.

Pastor Bobby Davis and First Lady Bernice Davis

Inspiration: The late Pastor Doyle Lane Jr., my spiritual brother and Overseer Essie Lane-Fox

Encouragement: Clara, Sandra, Tammy and Fussell

CPSIA information can be obtained
at www.ICGtesting.com
Printed in the USA
FFOW04n1905200615
14445FF